Introduction

The **Harcourt Electronic Test System** is a revolutionary approach to in-class practice and assessment. There are two major components to the program. The **Teacher Edition** serves as the teacher's assignment planner, grade book, and instructional management system. The **Student Edition** provides online tests and practice activities. Together, the **Teacher** and **Student Editions** function as:

A Computer-Administered Testing and Practice Program that provides:
- Online test-taking with automatic scoring.
- Tests and assignments that correspond to the assessment and practice items in *Harcourt Horizons*.
- A bank of items from which teachers can build their own practice activities.
- Immediate feedback on students' performance. Teachers may choose to block students' access to correct answers until all students have completed an assignment.
- A wide variety of item types, including multiple-choice, fill-in-the-blank, all-that-apply, drop-down, and essay (or extended answer) formats.

An Instructional Management System that provides:
- Printable tests for traditional paper-and-pencil administration.
- Correlations of items to the textbook.
- Comprehensive program management and class reporting.
- Capability of importing class rosters.
- Tracking of each student's progress on particular objectives.

Schoolwide and districtwide upgrades are available for aggregating students' scores and providing school and district reports.

Social Studies Practice and Assessment

The **Harcourt Electronic Test System: Social Studies Practice and Assessment** CD-ROMs contain electronic versions of the tests and practice activities developed to measure student achievement and reinforce the skills taught in *Harcourt Horizons*. For each book, there is a corresponding CD. Each CD contains the following tests and practice activities:

Tests adapted from the *Harcourt Assessment* component of *Harcourt Horizons*:
- Unit Assessments
- Chapter Assessments

Chapter Review/Tests are adapted from the **Student Edition** and are available as an itembank from which teachers can select individual questions to build their own assignments.

Minimum System Requirements

This product can be installed as stand-alone or network software.

Workstations

Windows®
Intel® Pentium® 133MHz
Windows 98, 2000, ME, XP or Windows NT 4 Workstation
64 MB RAM
640x480, 800x600, or 1024x768 resolution
4x CD-ROM drive
75 MB hard drive space (stand-alone installation)
25 MB hard drive space (network installation)

Macintosh®
Power PC, G3, G4 or iMac®
Mac OS 8.1 - OS 10.2.2 (Classic Mode), (For OS 10 clients
connecting to a Novell® network server: OS 10.2 required)
64 MB RAM
640x480 to 824x632 resolution
(Does not support millions of colors)
4x CD-ROM drive
150 MB hard drive space (stand-alone installation)
25 MB hard drive space (network installation)

Network Servers

Windows NT
Windows NT 4.0
Pentium 166 server with 64 MB RAM
4x CD-ROM drive
Ethernet® 10/100
75 MB hard drive space (Windows)
180 MB hard drive space (Macintosh and Windows)

Windows 2000/2003 Server
Windows 2000/2003 server
Pentium 166 server with 128 MB RAM
4x CD-ROM drive
Ethernet 10/100
75 MB hard drive space (Windows)
180 MB hard drive space (Macintosh and Windows)

Macintosh AppleShare®
AppleShare 4.2.1
Power Mac® server with 64 MB RAM
4x CD-ROM drive
Ethernet NIC 10/100
150 MB hard drive space (Macintosh)

Novell® NetWare®
Novell NetWare 4.0
Pentium 166 server with 64 MB RAM
4x CD-ROM drive
Ethernet 10/100
75 MB hard drive space (Windows)
180 MB hard drive space (Macintosh and Windows)

Stand-Alone Installation

Teacher Edition on a Windows Workstation

1. Insert the CD-ROM into the CD-ROM drive.
2. Double-click the **My Computer** icon on your desktop.
3. Double-click the **Electronic Test System CD-ROM** icon.
4. Double-click the set-up icon for the program that you would like to install.
5. Read the welcome screen and click **Next** to continue.
6. The next screen is the registration screen. Enter your registration information in the space provided. Click **OK** to continue.
7. Select Local Stand-Alone Installation. Click **OK** to continue.
8. In the Destination Location Screen, select the location on your computer where you want the software installed. The default is **C:\Harcourt\Electronic Test System**.
9. Select the location on your computer where you want the program icon to be stored. The default location is **Harcourt Horizons I Electronic Test System** inside the **Programs** folder on the Start menu.
10. Read the licensing agreement. If you agree with the terms outlined here, click **Yes** to continue. If you do not, click **No** and contact your sales representative.
11. Select all of the components that you would like to install. Make sure that **Teacher Edition** is checked.
12. Follow the instructions on screen to complete the installation.

Student Edition on a Windows Workstation

1. Follow the directions above, up to step 11, for the **Teacher Edition**.
2. Make sure that **Student Edition** is checked and that **Teacher Edition** is not checked. Follow the instructions on the screen to complete the installation.

Teacher Edition on a Macintosh Workstation

1. Insert the CD-ROM into the CD-ROM drive.
2. Double-click the **Electronic Test System** CD-ROM icon.
3. Double-click the **Harcourt Electronic Test System** set-up icon.
4. Read the welcome screen and click **Continue**.
5. Read the licensing agreement. If you agree with the terms outlined here, click **Accept** to continue. If you do not, click **Decline** and contact your sales representative.
6. Review the Readme file. Click **Continue** to move on.
7. The next screen is the registration screen. Enter your registration information in the space provided. Click **Register** to continue.
8. Select Local Stand-Alone Installation. Click **OK** to continue.
9. Select all of the components that you would like to install. Make sure that **Teacher Edition** is checked. Follow the instructions on screen to complete the installation.

Student Edition on a Macintosh Workstation

1. Follow the directions above, up to step 9, for the **Teacher Edition**.
2. Make sure that **Student Edition** is checked and that **Teacher Edition** is not checked. Follow the instructions on the screen to complete the installation.

Network Installation

The license allows for a network installation of this product. To use the network version, you must first install the program on your server (ensure you have proper network administration permissions). Then install the program on each client machine. If you are installing to a mixed network (Windows and Mac clients), install both to the same drive location on the server FROM A MACINTOSH. It is highly recommended that a network administrator perform this installation.

Windows or Novell Network Server and Client Installations

Installing to a Windows or Novell Network

1. Insert the CD-ROM into the CD-ROM drive.
2. Double-click the **My Computer** icon on the desktop.
3. Double-click the **Electronic Test System** CD-ROM icon.
4. Double-click the set-up icon to launch the installation.
5. Read the welcome screen and click **Next** to continue.
6. The next screen is the registration screen. Enter your registration information in the space provided. Click **OK** to continue.
7. Select Network Server Installation. Click **OK** to continue.
8. On the Destination Location screen, click **Browse** to select a drive letter that is mapped to the network. Choose the drive letter where you want your program icon stored and click **OK**.
9. Verify that the drive letter appears in the Destination Directory box. Click **Next** to continue.
10. Click **OK** to install the program to the drive letter and add the default directory to complete the installation path.
11. Verify that the full installation path appears in the Destination Directory box. The default path begins with the drive letter, for example, **D:\Harcourt\Electronic Test System**.
   Click **Next** to continue.
12. Read the licensing agreement. If you agree with the terms outlined here, click **Yes** to continue. If you do not, click **No** and contact your sales representative.
13. Make sure that all components are checked. Click **Next**.
14. Follow the instructions on screen to complete the installation.

Installing to a Windows Client Machine from a Windows or Novell Server

1. Make sure the client machine is properly mapped to the server.
2. Locate and double-click the directory on the network server that contains the software. The default path begins with the drive letter, for example, **D:\Harcourt\ElectronicTest System**. Note: For users of the Single Teacher license of this software, the software creates a sub-folder for each user at this level.
3. Double-click the **Setup_WIN_Workstation.exe** icon.
4. Read the welcome screen and click **Next** to continue.
5. The next screen is the registration screen. Enter your registration information in the space provided. Click **OK** to continue.
6. Choose a destination directory where you would like to install the software. Click **Next** to continue.
7. Read the licensing agreement. If you agree with the terms outlined here, click **Yes** to continue. If you do not, click **No** and contact your sales representative.
8. Select all of the components that you would like to install. Make sure that **Teacher Edition** and **Student Edition** are checked. Click **Next**.
9. Select the program folder that will store the program icon. The default is **Harcourt Horizons I Electronic Test System** inside the Programs folder on the Start menu. Click **Next** to continue and follow the instructions on the screen to complete the installation.

Student Edition on a Windows Client Machine

1. Follow the directions above, up to step 8, for the **Teacher Edition**.
2. Make sure that **Student Edition** is checked and that **Teacher Edition** is not checked. Follow the instructions on the screen to complete the installation.

Installing to a Windows® or Novell® Server from a MacOS Client Machine

1. Insert the CD-ROM into the CD-ROM drive.
2. Double-click the **Electronic Test System** CD-ROM icon.
3. Double-click the set-up icon.
4. Read the welcome screen and click **Continue**.
5. Read the licensing agreement. If you agree with the terms outlined here, click **Accept** to continue. If you do not, click **Decline** and contact your sales representative.
6. Review the Readme file. Click **Continue** to move on.
7. The next screen is the registration screen. Enter your registration information in the space provided. Click **Register** to continue.
8. Select Server Installation. Click **OK**.
9. Make sure all components are checked. In the Install Location box, choose the location where you would like to install the software. Click **Install** to continue.

Installing to a Macintosh® Server from a MacOS Client Machine

1. Insert the CD-ROM into the CD-ROM drive.
2. Double-click the **Electronic Test System** CD-ROM icon.
3. Double-click the set-up icon.
4. Read the welcome screen and click **Next** to continue.
5. Read the licensing agreement. If you agree with the terms outlined here, click **Accept** to continue. If you do not, click **Decline** and contact your sales representative.
6. Review the Readme file. Click **Continue** to move on.
7. The next screen is the registration screen. Enter your registration information in the space provided. Click **Register** to continue.
8. Select Server Installation. Click **OK**.
9. Make sure all components are checked. In the Install Location box, choose the destination directory where you would like to install the software. Click **Install** to continue.

Installing to a Macintosh Client Machine from a MacOS Server

Teacher Edition on a Macintosh Client Machine

1. Make sure the client machine is properly mapped to the server.
2. Locate and double-click the folder that contains the software. The default location is **Harcourt\Electronic Test System**. Note: For users of the Single Teacher version, the software will create an individual sub-folder with the teacher's name at this level.
3. Locate and double-click the **Setup_MAC_Workstation.exe** program to start the installation.
4. Read the welcome screen and click **Continue**.
5. Read the licensing agreement. If you agree with the terms outlined here, click **Accept** to continue. If you do not, click **Decline** and contact your sales representative.
6. Review the Readme file. Click **Continue** to move on.
7. The next screen is the registration screen. Enter your registration information in the space provided. Click **Register** to continue.
8. Make sure all components are checked. In the Install Location box, choose the location where you would like to install the software. Click **Install** to complete the installation.

Student Edition on a Macintosh® Client Machine

1. Follow the directions above, up to step 8, for the **Teacher Edition**.
2. Make sure that **Student Edition** is checked and that **Teacher Edition** is not checked. Follow the instructions on the screen to complete the installation.

Using the Teacher Edition

To access the **Teacher Edition** on a Windows workstation, go to the **Start** menu. From there, select **Programs | Harcourt Horizons | Electronic Test System | Teacher Edition**. In the Single Teacher version of this software, teachers double-click the folder labeled with their name.

To access the **Teacher Edition** on a Macintosh workstation, open the **Electronic Test System** folder on your desktop and double-click the **Teacher Edition** icon. In the Single Teacher version of this software, teachers double-click the icon labeled with their name.

Teacher ID

If this is the first time that you have used the program, click **New User** on the sign-in screen.

1. Enter a Teacher ID (up to ten characters) and your name.
2. It is important to password-protect teachers' access to the **Teacher Edition**. As soon as you reach the Bulletin Board screen, click the **Change Preferences** box.
3. Select Teacher Password and follow the directions on the screen.

A Guide to the Bulletin Board

The Bulletin Board serves as the main menu for the **Teacher Edition**. Before you can assign tests and practice activities, you must set up your classes and enroll students. The following material will guide you through these steps and help you use the product for the first time. For additional information and guidance, please refer to the **Need Help** button on the right-hand side of this screen.

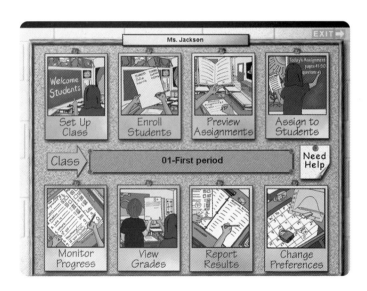

Set Up Class

1. To begin, a class must be entered into the system. To do so, click the Set Up Class icon. You may add up to eight classes per teacher.
2. Choose **New Class**.
3. In the **New Class Information** window, enter a description for the class.
4. Select a default **Content Library**. You may give assignments from any content library. **United States History**, for example, contains tests that correspond to the print materials in *Harcourt Horizons*. **My Content Library** contains assignments that you build yourself from a bank of items.
5. Select a default **Curriculum Map**. To see the table of contents for your textbook, select the program (or title) you are using.

Enroll Students

(If you want to import a class roster, do so from the **Change Preferences** box.)

1. Select **Add** to add students to the new class. Students may be added or deleted from the system at any time. You may add up to fifty students per class.
2. Enter a unique student ID, name, and password for each student.

Preview
Assignments

Preview Assignments

Here you may view an assignment, build your own assignment using questions from the item bank, and print paper-and-pencil tests and answer keys.

- **View an Assignment**

    Select **Content Library** to view a menu of prebuilt tests from *Harcourt Horizons*. To view an assignment that you built, select **My Content Library**. Then select the assignment by the title you gave to it.

- **Build an Assignment**

    1. Select the item bank that you would like to use, for example, **United States History**.
    2. Select the **Curriculum Map** you would like to use. To see where the items correspond to *Harcourt Horizons*'s table of contents, select the textbook you are using.
    3. Enter a topic description for **My Content Library**.
    4. Follow the instructions on the screen to select your items.
    5. In the Save dialog box, enter a title for your assignment. Then click **OK**.

Assign to Students

This feature places assignments in the **Student Edition**. To assign a test or practice activity for electronic administration and scoring, follow these steps:

1. Click **Add** on the **List of Assignments**.
2. Select the **Content Library** and assignment you would like to use. To assign a test from *Harcourt Horizons*, select a **Harcourt Horizons's** title, for example **People and Communities**. Then select the test you would like to assign. To assign material you assembled yourself, select **My Content Library**. Then find the practice activities that you made.
3. Choose a start date for the assignment. Assignments will not appear in the **Student Edition** before this date. Then choose an end date.
4. If you would like to time the test, click **Yes** on the **Timed Test** option. Then enter the number of minutes.
5. Determine the scoring weight of the assignment and whether the assignment should appear in the students' grade report.
6. If you do not want students to review the results after they have completed the assignment, click **No** on the **Student View Results** option.
7. Then click **Save**. When the assignment appears on the **List of Assignments**, click **Close**.

Monitor Progress

Here you can monitor student's status, review student's results, enter comments on their assigned and completed work, adjust scores, and reassign assignments. This is also where you review and enter the scores of essays and open response answers that cannot be scored electronically.

View Grades

Once students have completed assignments, you can view a summary of their results here. Select a student's name from the drop-down list to view scores on graded assignments. This screen also shows the overall average score and letter grade. Go to **Report Results** to see detailed grade information and to print reports.

Report Results

Report Results

Here you can view and print reports on students' results. Select the type of report from the drop-down list. The available reports are:

- **Student Grade Report** – Displays the list of assignments each student has completed, the student's score, the weight of the assignment, and the letter grade.
- **Student Assignment Report** – Displays the list of assignments completed by each student, the number of items correct, the number of items attempted, the average score, the date completed, and the elapsed time.
- **Student Objective Report** – Displays the student's name, the objective descriptions, the objective codes, the number of items the student completed that measured each objective, the number of those possible items that the student answered correctly, and a score for each objective measured.
- **Student Gain Report** – Tracks student progress on objectives that are tested multiple times.
- **Student Mastery Report** – Reports to the teacher whether the student is below mastery, has partially mastered, or has mastered all of the tested objective standards.
- **Class Grade Report** – Displays the list of assignments given to a class, the names of all students in the class, their scores for each assignment, and the class average for each assignment.
- **Class Assignment Report** – Displays the list of assignments given to a class. It also shows the students' names with their score for each assignment and the class average per assignment.

- **Class Assignment Summary** – Displays the list of assignments given to a class, the number of items per assignment, the class average per assignment, the number of students each assignment has been given to, and the number of students who have completed the assignments.
- **Class Mastery Report** – Creates a list of tested objectives for the class. This list indicates whether the class average is below mastery, partially mastered, or mastered. It also provides the class average for each standard.
- **Class Mastery Summary** – Similar to the Class Mastery Report. The Class Mastery Summary reports the tested objectives and the class mastery level for each objective. In addition the Class Mastery Summary provides cluster averages.
- **Class Objective Report** – Displays the list of objectives that were measured for a class, the entire list of students in the class, each student's score on each objective, and a class average for each objective.
- **Class Objective Summary** – Displays the objective descriptions, the objective codes, and the class's average score for each objective.

Change
Preferences

Change Preferences

Here you can enter or change the system's marking periods and grade table, as well as your teacher ID, name, and password.
You can also import a class roster and export students' assignment results to programs such as Crystal Reports® and Microsoft® Excel.

Synchronizing Data for Stand-Alone Use

Teachers using this product on stand-alone machines must synchronize teacher and student data. After the software has been installed on the teacher and student machines, complete the following tasks:

1. Build classes and assign work to students.
2. Select **Synchronize Data** from the **Change Preferences** menu on the Bulletin Board. Place a diskette into the diskette drive. This routine will copy the data information onto the diskette.
3. Insert the diskette into student machines and log into the student software using your teacher ID.
4. Select **Syncronize Data** and click **OK.**
5. Select **Yes** on the **Synchronize Files** message.
6. Repeat on all student machines.
7. When students have completed assignments, insert the disk in the student machines and log in using your teacher ID.
8. Select **Syncronize Data** and click **OK.**
9. Select **Yes** on the **Synchronize Files** message.
10. Insert the diskette into your machine and choose **Synchronize Data** from the **Change Preferences** menu. The system will automatically copy the necessary files from the diskette onto your hard drive.

Using the Student Edition

To access the **Student Edition** on a Windows workstation, go to the **Start** menu. From there, select **Programs | Harcourt Horizons | Electronic Test System | Student Edition**. In the Single Teacher version of this software, students double-click the folder labeled with their teacher's name.

To access the **Student Edition** on a Macintosh workstation, open the **Electronic Test System** folder on your desktop and double-click the **Student Edition** icon. In the Single Teacher version of this software, students double-click the icon labeled with their teacher's name.

Student ID

Each student signs into the **Student Edition** by entering the unique **Student ID** and **Password** assigned to them by their teacher. Once a student has signed in, the screen displays their personal list of assignments.

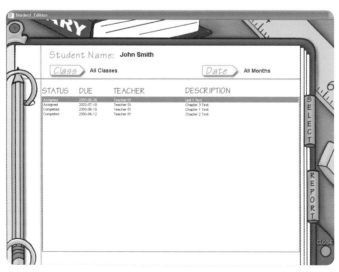

Assignments appear in a student's notebook once the start date has commenced.

The left-hand column indicates the student's progress on an assignment.

- "Assigned" means that the student has not started the assignment.
- "In progress" means that the student has started, but has not finished the assignment.
- "Submitted" means that the student has finished the assignment, but you need to score any essay or open response answers.
- "Completed" means that the student has finished the assignment and that the assignment has been scored.

Completing Assignments

To complete or review an assignment, a student clicks the assignment in the notebook, then clicks the **Select** tab.
Each assignment consists of a variety of item types, including:

- **Standard Multiple Choice** – A set of possible answer choices are displayed with A, B, C, D answer boxes in front of them. Students select their answer by clicking on the correct box.
- **Multiple Choice Circle** – Circles display around possible answers as students move their cursor across an item. Students select the correct answer by clicking on it.
- **All That Apply Circle** – Circles display around possible answers as students move their cursor across an item. Students select the correct answers by clicking on them.
- **Fill in the Blank** – Allows students to type correct answers into a text box.
- **Drop Down** – Students click on a blue drop down box to display a list of possible responses. Students select the correct response by clicking on it.
- **Essay** – Allows students to type an extended answer into a text box. These items are teacher scored.
- **Multiple Item Types** – The software allows for any combination of the above item types.

Student Progress

Students may review their progress on assignments by clicking the **Report** tab. Clicking the numbered button will display the assignments' title and score.

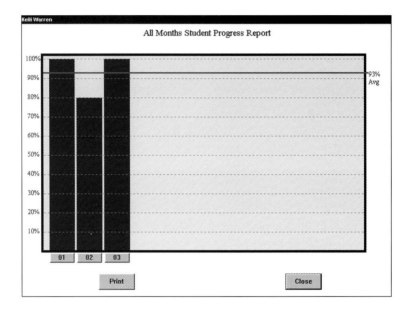

Program Maintenance and Uninstall

It is highly recommended that a network administrator perform the uninstall.

Windows
1. Open the Control Panels window under Settings on the Windows Start menu.
2. Double-click **Add/Remove Programs**.
3. Find the **Harcourt Electronic Test System** software subject and grade level that you would like to remove and highlight it.
4. Click **Remove**.

The uninstall only removes subject and grade-level-specific content. To remove all remaining software, including student and teacher records, you must drag the folders to the system recycle bin.

Macintosh
Simply drag the **Electronic Test System** folder that you would like to remove to the trash can. **Caution**: This will remove all teacher and student records.

Technical Help

If you experience difficulties installing or running this software, please contact Harcourt Technical Support using one of the numbers below:

Technology Service Hotline
1-800-419-3900

Interactive Technical Support on the Web
www.harcourtschool.com/support

Customer Service

For questions concerning your order, to order additional products, or to request a catalog, please call Customer Service at 1-800-225-5425 or visit **The Market Place** on the Web at www.harcourtschool.com/marketplace.